WHERE HE LEADS,
I WILL FOLLOW

WHERE HE LEADS, I WILL FOLLOW

AN AUTOBIOGRAPHY

REV. JOSEPH J. CUOCO

WESTBOW°
PRESS
A DIVISION OF THOMAS NELSON
& ZONDERVAN

WestBow Press books may be ordered through booksellers or by contacting:
WestBow Press
A Division of Thomas Nelson & Zondervan
1663 Liberty Drive
Bloomington, IN 47403
www.westbowpress.com
1 (866) 928-1240

All scripture references are in NKJV, except where noted.

ISBN: 978-1-4908-3892-2 (sc)
ISBN: 978-1-4908-3893-9 (e)

Library of Congress Control Number: 2014909628

Printed in the United States of America.

WestBow Press rev. date: 08/06/2014

DEDICATION

I dedicate this book to our precious Lord Jesus, who loves us with an everlasting love, and has called us with an everlasting call, and graciously declared: "Without Me you can do nothing!" PTL!!!

I lovingly dedicate this book to my dear Wife Herborg, she has been at my side throughout the years of our ministry. Truly, the Lord has spoken numerous times to her, and it has come to pass. Herborg has been a great supporter, encourager and prayer warrior. Without her, we could not have accomplished the work to which we were called.

I would also like to dedicate this book to our Children, Grandchildren, Great Grandchildren, Sons-in-law and Daughter-in-law...my Beautiful Family!!!

Finally, I dedicate this book to my daughter Laila, who lovingly devoted her time and talent in this journey as I wrote this book.

PREFACE

It was the summer of 2006 while spending quality time with, our family in Norway. I had just returned from the ministry in Kenya, Africa. At that time, the Holy Spirit began to press upon my heart that I should publish a book, autobiography, a detailed report that would explain "how it all began." A testimony that declares, "How GREAT IS OUR GOD!!!"

This book will include our background before we came to Christ, and our ongoing ministry after we received Christ.

The Lord made clear to me that this book must describe the way He "led" us, and the "way" we followed. It must describe in detail, the miracles demonstrated, and His power revealed. And, it must be supported by scriptures- the Word of God!

In reading this book my prayer is that it will be a reminder to the believer, and open the eyes of a skeptic that God has not changed. What He does for others, He will do for you. His only demand is that we believe. "But without faith it impossible to please Him, for he who comes to God must believe that he is and that He is a rewarder of those who diligently seek HIM" (Heb. 11:6).

Open your heart to believing and receiving the things God has prepared for you so that you too can proclaim "Where He leads I will follow..."

INTRODUCTION

The purpose of this book is to demonstrate the plan of God in our lives. As our Creator, Designer, and Architect, He fashions us into the image of His dear Son. As sons and daughters, we have been called to bring forth fruit according to His will and for His glory. Truly, the Lord has a perfect plan for each Christian to fulfill however; it must start with the first step, trust and obey. The Lord says, "I will bless the work of your hands and you will be a blessing"! His purpose and plan cannot be fulfilled without us and so He invites us to share in His plan.

I have discovered that the majority of Christians have no idea as to the leading of the Holy Spirit, hearing His still small voice, and obeying His command to "Follow Me". My prayer is that this book will inspire you to become more in tune with His leading, making it easier to follow, which will allow you to experience the many adventures & complete plan God has for your life.

1

HOW IT ALL BEGAN

The plan of God for our lives all started years ago. My Wife (Herborg) was born and raised in Norway. Her parents were Godly people and well seasoned in the power of prayer. During the period of WW2, the Nazi's took over Norway. Herborg's Father was a shoemaker by trade, and refused to cooperate with the Nazis. They wanted him to make boots for the Nazi soldiers, but he refused. As a result, they took over his store, and he was confined to a concentration camp, but by the grace of God he had escaped. After many days, he successfully made his way back home.

As the years passed Herborg went to Bible School, and eventually, moved to America, Brooklyn, NY to be exact. She was not serving the Lord at that time, so she had no idea this was the "master plan" of the Lord. She found a Norwegian community in Brooklyn and settled there. Now, I pause here to remind you that God takes pleasure in fashioning and forming a people for

Himself, as a Master Designer who sees and declares "the end from the beginning". Interestingly, I happen to be born and raised in Brooklyn, NY nearby the area of this Norwegian community. But who would know this? After all, who could plan all the details, timing, and location for us to meet? And who could create a scenario, whereby our paths would cross in the city of 8 million? I am beginning to see this is no coincidence, but the hand of the Lord.

Herborg, her friends, and much of the Norwegian populous enjoyed Country Western Music. It just so happened that my brother and I loved to play that genre of music. In fact, at the time we played in a Country Western band in a night club circle. Now let me call your attention to the fact that it is highly unlikely for two teenage boys to enjoy this kind of music having been raised in Brooklyn during the sixty's. "For my thoughts are not your thoughts, nor are your ways My ways," says the Lord (Is.55:8). And His plan is still on track.

In the process of time, my Brother, the band, & I were invited to perform at the Sons of Norway, in Brooklyn. And of course, Herborg happened to be there (are you beginning to suspect something?). Is this none other than the Lord bringing about His Master Plan for our lives?

2

OUR WEDDING, PLANS, & ADVENTURE

Our wedding day had finally arrived on April 23, 1966 after two years of courting my beautiful Norwegian bride. Of course, we had no idea what this union of adventure would bring. But, there is only One who could possibly orchestrate this plan and carry out such vivid details for a non- fiction love story as this.

We began this new chapter in our lives not knowing the Lord. But, the Lord knew the plans He had for us: "Having called us from our mother's womb, and foreordained us that we should bring forth fruit for His glory. " For I know the thoughts that I have towards you says the Lord, thoughts of peace and not of evil, to give you a future and a hope" (Jer. 29:11).

3

Our Honeymoon

Our honeymoon day had arrived and as planned we began our journey from Brooklyn, NY with intentions of going to Alaska (a one year Honeymoon trip) in our Jeep and trailer. Both of us having a pioneer spirit seeking adventure were very excited! Is the Lord still directing us? I believe He may not have been in every detail at this time, but His plan for our lives is still on tract. I remind you when it is required to make a correction along the way; the Lord in His infinite wisdom lovingly moves us in the right direction without our knowledge.

We finally arrived in L.A. California when suddenly our Jeep needed some very major repairs. Financially we did not have much left. Finding ourselves in this dilemma, we decided to seek employment. We applied for a position with an agent, and we were happily placed as a couple in the home of Jack Warner of Warner Brothers Studios, Beverly Hills. Herborg was placed as second cook, and I was placed as one of their gardeners. Neither of us had the experience. Nevertheless, we had favor with all and happily served in that capacity for some time. In the process of time having gained some experience, we secured the same position with another movie producer named Saul West of Bel Air, Ca. It wasn't what we planned for our Honeymoon, but certainly turned out to be quite the adventure!!

Eventually, we were able to purchase a new Land Rover, resigned our positions, and continued to enjoy the rest of our honeymoon. After the year was up we made our way back to Brooklyn, NY where we moved in with my parents. In the mean time, my former position as Steel Engineer was available and waiting for me (was this the hand of the Lord?).

4

The Adventure Continues

F ast forwarding, we are now in Moscow, Idaho with an engineering firm that offered me a position in which I accepted, and we relocated. You may ask, "Moscow, Idaho! Why??" Besides being transferred there for work, the Lord had other plans as well. He had situated His first witness to introduce the Gospel to me. He used my supervisor's wife, thereby, a seed was sown and being watered. It was also during this time; Herborg gave birth to our first child, Laila.

After a period of time, I had completed my project for the company, and my time in Moscow, Idaho had come to an end. I was then transferred back to the East Coast, where we eventually moved back to Brooklyn, NY and returned to my former company and position in NYC. In hindsight, we now see the hand of the Lord directing us back to my former employer as Steel Engineer for a reason. Let me mention, if I haven't already, that some Christians would conclude that this can't be the hand of the Lord, since God does not lead and provide for unbelievers. (I will let the Theologians argue this one.)

Another big surprise, we had the happy occasion of Herborg giving birth to our second child, Christina, who was born in Brooklyn, NY. ("Where He leads us, He will guide us".) Unaware of His Sovereign hand, the day draws closer to the Lord. "For who has known the mind of the Lord…?" (Rom.11:34).

During our stay with my parents, we finally found a home to move into. So we moved from Brooklyn to Hasbrouck Heights, NJ. We would now be raising our family in a rural area, and I was still able to commute to NYC while maintaining my present position as Steel Engineer in NYC.

The Lord continued to bless us with our third child, Joseph John. The Holy Spirit was busy putting the pieces of the puzzle together. For the Master Designer and builder takes pleasure in His creation. "Oh the depth of the riches both of the wisdom and knowledge of God! How unsearchable are His judgments and His ways past finding out!" (Rom.11:33).

5

A GODLY SETBACK

We are now settled in our new beautiful home which included an Olympic size heated pool. Then suddenly, I was notified that my company was cutting back and laying off. This prompted me to switch to another construction company in NYC. This was a major transition for me, as we viewed it to be an unwelcome change for our family, as well. However, in God's eyes, this detour was right on tract, and according to His perfect plan. In fact, He was positioning us for that glorious day where Herborg & I would give our hearts & lives to the Lord. Needless to say, we had no clue as to His plan. He was the pilot; we were on board for the ride!

Having now made the transition to my new job, invariably, my time spent on the job became very precious to me, for it was here that I met Al

Christiansen, my fellow co-worker on assignment from the Lord to introduce me to Christ. (I don't think he was aware of this at the time.) One day during lunch, we were discussing the things of God and the Bible, and Al would answer my questions from the Bible. Consequently, this was the beginning of my quest and thirst for the things of God.

6

OUR ENCOUNTER WITH OUR CREATOR

"Behold, I will do a new thing and shall you know it"

Our daily lunch hour at times became a mini Bible study. Al, having served the Lord for many years, perceived that the Lord's hand was in this and that I was ready to receive Christ. My dear friend Al Christiansen had a plan, which of course was the Holy Spirit directing him or might I say, "calling the shots." (Here again, we are about to see the plan of God unfolding in a mystery.) The Lord: "Declaring the end from the beginning."

Herborg, having been raised in Norway was naturally drawn to the Norwegian culture and people. And of course, this was no surprise to the Lord but in fact, very much part of His plan. When He situated me on this job site, he also situated Al Christiansen to be at the same job site. (Are you ready for this?) Al "happened" to be Norwegian, and his wife Aslaug happened to be born in Norway. Are you beginning to see the Lord's plan unfold? "Who has known the mind of the Lord? Or who has become His counselor?" (Rom.11:34).

As the Lord's plan continues to unfold, Al and his wife Aslaug were busy planning, as well. Having now invited us to their home in Long Island for a weekend. It should be no surprise that this weekend was orchestrated by the Holy Spirit. And, of course Herborg found it easy to accept the invitation, since she was drawn to her Norwegian people and culture.

The hour had now arrived: And during that glorious weekend, Feb.28, 1973, when in the late evening, in their living room while I was asleep, Aslaug shared Christ with Herborg and led her into the prayer of salvation. When suddenly, I awoke to Herborg's weeping, and at that moment the Holy Spirit said "This is what you have been searching for." I knelt beside my wife, and we were gloriously born again.

Our search was over, (but unbeknown to us just the beginning). We discovered that we were now complete in HIM!!! Truly, we had experienced what the Scriptures declare when it says, "If any man is in Christ, he is a new creation, old things have passed away, behold, all things have become new" (2 Cor.5:17).

7

A New Day-A New Life

Suddenly, our former lifestyle had lost its glamour. We became to it as Paul declared dead to the things of the world, and alive to His new creation, to His kingdom, to His purpose, and most of all to Christ Himself!! His plan and purpose became our focus day and night. We couldn't get enough of His Word, His love, His knowledge, and fellowship with like believers. We were like two kids set free in a candy factory. Al and Aslaug quickly directed us to a church in our community where we began to grow in His grace, and feeding on His Word daily. "And they continued steadfastly in the apostles' doctrine and fellowship, in the breaking of bread, and in prayer" (Acts 2:42). Truly, this was a new day and a new life for us in Christ!!

8

THE BAPTISM IN THE HOLY SPIRIT

It's clear in the scriptures (Acts 1:4-5), that the promise of the Father that Jesus spoke of was referring to the gift of the Holy Spirit. He also promised when the Holy Spirit comes; He will make you witnesses. (Acts 1:8) And as they waited for the promise of the Holy Spirit in the upper room, He came upon them after ten days as promised (Acts 2:1-4).

And what was the evidence of the coming Holy Spirit? "They were all filled with the Holy Spirit and began to speak in other tongues as the Spirit gave them utterance." Now, what is the evidence today to receiving the Holy Spirit? You will speak in tongues!!

How do I qualify to receive this gift? First, you must be born again, second, you must believe that the gift is for you, third, you must receive the gift by faith, fourth, you must begin to speak as the Spirit gives you utterance (words). Consequently, I began to search and ask as a baby Christian. But, my wife Herborg was one who did not wait for the gift. She simply received the gift at the time she was saved (born again).

Nevertheless, I had taken every opportunity to have hands laid on me. I was patient and persevered. I was asking, seeking, and knocking to receive the gift. And that glorious day finally arrived when I received the gift: It was during our home fellowship which we had weekly. That evening we happened to have two evangelists visiting from another Country. I had them lay hands on me, and I began to speak in other tongues.

Now for those who desire the gift. It's yours!!!

9

THE CALL

During this joyful time in the grace of God and in serving the Lord, we were once again blessed with our fourth child Elisa. As for us, our quiver was quite full! It was during this time that we began to sense the call of God to full time ministry. I remind you of His word: "Declaring the end from the beginning" (Is.46:10) is in the process of fulfillment. "For the gifts and the calling of God are irrevocable" (Rom.11:29).

We began to seek the Lord for His plan and direction. There was a strong stirring in our hearts, so we began to seek counsel with our Pastor, friends, and our spiritual parents. During this process of time, we came to the conclusion that this was the Lord. Therefore, we began to make plans to sell our home and relocate to a Bible College in Greenville, Pa. I applied; I was accepted, and at the same time, our home was placed with a Realtor.

We were doing all we knew to do in obeying the call of God on our lives. And we began packing our belongings as we anticipated our departure.

As time went on, we faced our first trial. That is, we found ourselves living out of our suitcase. As a result, we began to doubt our call. We believed we heard from the Holy Spirit. Our house was still on the market. Our plans were conceivably put on hold. As young Christians, we grew frustrated, then disillusioned. We began to question God. "Why are you letting this happen?"

10

UNEXPECTED VISITOR

As we were approaching Labor Day, 1975. We made a decision before the Lord: that if our house was not sold by Labor Day, we would cancel our plans for Bible College. (Unaware this was from the Lord.) As Labor Day arrived, there was a knock on our door. A lady "happened to be driving by" and saw the "for sale" sign for our home. We invited her in; she viewed our home once, and decided to purchase it. "Now this is the Lord's doing, it is marvelous in our eyes" (Psm.118:23).

The Lord had more in mind...this same family who purchased our home also received the Lord in our home!! ("His mercy endures forever.")

11

HOUSE SHOPPING

Our next step was to locate a house in proximity to the Bible College. Now after seeking the Lord for direction, we made our way to Pennsylvania, and as we approached the area, we noticed a Realtor nearby. ("Where He leads, we will follow.") To our surprise, he was also a Christian whose name was JR. After sharing our testimony with him, he was encouraged to help us. Shortly thereafter, JR located a house which fit our families' needs, having four children. JR directed us to the Bank, whose manager happened to be a Christian also. (Could this be the Lord?)

"I will guide you with my eyes." And again, having shared our testimony with the manager (We will call him John), as well as our need for a mortgage John determined that we did not qualify. His decision was based on our present status: We were unemployed with no promise of employment, having a family of six with little or no assets. On top of that, we were from out of state, and a full time college student. (This was a recipe for rejection).

Was there any good news in his report? Yes! John went on to say that, in his heart, he had made a decision contrary to bank rules to approve the loan. ("I will even make a road in the wilderness...") (Is.43:19).

I was well on my way to Bible College to begin my first semester, January, 1976, preparing myself for full time ministry. "For as many as are led by the Spirit of God, these are the sons of God" (Rom.8:14).

12

UNEXPECTED MOVE

W e were now settled in our new home; our children situated in their new school, and I had begun my classes. Suddenly, the student body of our College was notified that a transition was about to take place. The College administration was offered the property from the US Army hospital as a grant. The property had been vacated and available for the College to assume. This grant, which was a gift, would provide the college with 72 acres and many buildings to occupy.

However, for the students with families, this would become a burden and added expense. We were left with two choices: either, commute 30 miles one way, or relocate to the campus area. Consequently, we cried out to the LORD. We questioned Him as to why He would send us here only to sell our house again and to relocate.

"For My thoughts are not your thoughts, nor are your ways My ways, says the Lord" (Is.55:8).

Having prayed, it seemed good before the Lord for us to relocate. Therefore, as we were approaching the summer months, we decided to look for an apartment or house in the college area. But we discovered the apartments were not available for a family of six. Moreover, the housing market was far more expensive than our current location. And again, we found ourselves in a dilemma, seemingly no way out. So what shall we do in a time of crises? We cried out to the Lord for help. And what was His answer "...I will even make a road in the wilderness..."(Is.43:19) Of course, the Lord had it all planned out. He wasn't taken by surprise with anything. He is the One who knows the end from the beginning.

During the spring semester, 1977 the college had relocated to its new campus and we were left to commute. And it came to pass, during that time, several students joined together to pray about our mutual dilemma since each had to commute, and each had a family of six. But the Lord was about to do a great thing for His glory, and to bring His plan to completion.

I am reminded, of David, when the Lord joined him together with a mighty army to do great exploits. So it was; the Lord joined us (these three families) together as one to do the same. He put us together, and we were given the opportunity to construct three apartments on campus with one of the vacated buildings. The Lord joined us together for such a time as this. Each one of us, students called of God, and uniquely equipped with skills and experience of their trade. One was a plumber, one an electrician, one a carpenter with architecture experience. Others joined to help with the labor, not to mention our wives who were always by our sides.

This vast project we had taken on was to be completed before the end of summer recess. What was our next step since we were running out of time? "Who can despise the day of small beginnings?" Our next step was to obtain permission from the College Administration. Subsequently, I drew up plans to one of the interior buildings, and then divided it into three apartments, each having three bedrooms. We then presented it to the administration.

Shortly thereafter, we received notice that our proposal was denied. Their concern was the apartments were too large, thereby, creating the appearance of favoritism. Well, back to the drawing board. (Now time is closing in on us.) While this is going on, my wife and the wives of each one were interceding. Now when my wife intercedes, something has to give!

Once again, we made some adjustment to the size of the apartments, the plans were again submitted. "Be anxious for nothing, but in everything by prayer and supplication with thanksgiving, let your request be made known to God…" (Phil.4:6). Shortly thereafter, the breakthrough had come, our prayers had been answered!

We received from the administration, their blessing to proceed! The agreement also stated that we may occupy the apartments after completion, and through graduation. And, we would only be responsible for the utilities. "And in everything give thanks, for this is the will of God in Christ Jesus for you." (1Thess.5:18).

13

PUTTING YOUR HAND TO THE PLOW

With no waste of time, we began construction on our new apartments. However, neither of us had resources to purchase the building material. As a result, we turned to our respective churches for help. And happily, they provided our needs.

But that's not all. We also discovered in some of these other U.S. Army vacated buildings, abandoned kitchen appliances, cabinets, and other items needed to complete the job all of which were in good condition. "And my God shall supply all of your need according to His riches in glory by Christ Jesus" (Phil.4:19).

We quickly "Put our hands to the plow and did not look back." Consequently, we spent 15-17 hours/ seven days a week, May-August to get the apartments completed. However, while this work was proceeding, our resources for my family were drying up. Moreover, our house that was up for sale was not sold. We made a conscience decision to request from the same banker John, for an extension on our loan. But as you recall, John approved the first loan contrary to Bank rules. Therefore, any extension would be a reflection on his judgment and record. Is this not another dilemma with any way out? (So we thought.) What was our Lord about to do?

About that time, we completed the construction of the three apartments in August, by the grace of God. And, surprisingly, the timing was perfect to begin our next semester. There was great excitement and celebration to see what the Lord had done! Nevertheless, the excitement quickly turned to frustration as we considered our house that was still on the market for several months, and our resources were near exhausted.

As we were waiting on the Lord for an answer, He clearly spoke to me saying, "When I sell your house will you give Me my tithe?" I quickly shared this with Herborg. And to my surprise, the Lord had asked her the same question while she was washing dishes. But her answer to the Lord was "If this is you Lord, you must ask my husband." And our answer was, "yes Lord."

Shortly thereafter, there was a knock on the door. The gentleman says he was from a certain Realtor. He offered to sell our house in a matter of two weeks or less. So, we agreed. And to our amazement, it was sold in less than two weeks. And even more amazing, unknowingly we would not see this man again. Who was this man? Where did he come from? How is it he knew our address? Who gave him permission to enter the college campus and ignore the security? Will we ever know?

Happily, our house was sold, and our friend John received his mortgage payoff. ("He does all things well".) God had seen us through once again. In return, Herborg & I agreed we would be a blessing to someone else in "need". One day during our Bible School chapel service Brother Grazer, our Professor, having returned from India during the summer break, began to share with the student body the financial need that one of our missionaries had. He was in need of finances in order to complete the Bible school there in India. Suddenly, the Holy Spirit said, "This is where you are to send your tithe." (And we did, according to His Word.) "Your ears shall hear a word behind you, saying, this is the way, walk in it…" (Is.30:21).

14

SCHOOLING FOR
THE CHILDREN

Our next challenge wasn't far ahead. We were faced with deciding our children's education, and which school to send our four children. We were told that the school in our community was overcrowded and unsafe. Again, we went to the Lord about this need. We were led to enroll them in a Christian School. However, we had no money for their tuition. But, by this time, we knew the Lord would make a way as He had many times before.

We had the opportunity to visit the school and to sit down with the principal. After having shared our testimony, we expressed our desire for our children to attend this particular school. But we went on to explain our financial dilemma of not having the tuition required.

Not surprisingly, he seemed somewhat puzzled. He replied, "What could you afford?" And I was somewhat embarrassed, as I blurted out "perhaps, fifty dollars a month" (not that we had that amount, and this of course was for four children). He replied, "We will let you know".

Now the start of the school year was upon us, and we had not heard from the Principal or the School Board. Disappointed, we escorted our children to the Public school on opening day. And to our great surprise, the Christian school contacted us the same day to inform us that our children were accepted. Now the Lord may be slow, but He is never late!! And, because of His faithfulness once again, my education, and the children's had been secured. "I know your works, See, I have set before you an open door, and no one can shut it..." (Rev.3:8).

15

THE GREAT PHYSICIAN

It was early in our Christian walk when the Holy Spirit began to reveal to us that Jesus is truly our healer. He provided our Salvation through His perfect work on the cross. This is clearly revealed in Isaiah 53:1-12, and in many other scriptures throughout the Bible. Having this knowledge and understanding, we set out to prove it as we confessed Jesus as our healer, and deliverer.

In my first semester, we were soon tested. Our youngest daughter Elisa, at the age of 18 months, suddenly came down with a high fever. We immediately brought her to the doctors. She was examined by our doctor who strongly recommended a spinal tap. Suddenly, the Holy Spirit emphatically said to me **"NO!"** I went with what I knew was God, and I declined the spinal tap, although our doctor strongly advised we do it. He of course, was not in agreement with our decision and replied, "you'll be back."

When we returned home there was a student from Bible College who happened to stop by. We told him what was going on and he joined us as we anointed Elisa with oil and laid hands on her according to the scriptures. She was instantly healed! The fever left, and we never had to return to the doctor's office.

Since that time, the Lord kept us in health throughout the years at the college campus. He demonstrated to us and to all who put their trust in HIM that He is **The Great Physician!** (Matt.8:16-17)

Let me share a great testimony of healing that I remember while going to Bible College: One evening several students had gathered for fellowship and prayer on campus at a friend's house. A student requested prayer for her mother who had been diagnosed with a terminal disease. As we held hands in a circle for prayer, my daughter who at the time was about age eleven joined us when suddenly, a white dove flew in through the window and landed on my daughter's shoulder. At that moment, my daughter said, "This dove is a messenger from God to tell you that your mother will be healed." And sure enough it was fulfilled as spoken, and came to pass!

16

JESUS OUR PROVIDER

There was another valuable lesson we learned when we put our trust in HIM. That is Jesus is our Provider. There are many scriptures to support this claim. When He multiplied the bread and fish, it says, "He had compassion on the multitude." His compassion is still new every morning for His children.

On numerous occasions, while attending Bible College, we found ourselves in need, and we discovered His creative ways of providing for us. On one occasion we found cash in our campus mail box, another time we found an envelope stuffed with cash under our front door, at other times, we were handed a check, or we discovered bags of groceries at the front door. We never mentioned our need to anyone, but simply believed God to provide while we were attending Bible College so that we could fulfill the call of God in our lives.

On another occasion, my Wife was in prayer, and she reminded the Lord of our needs. She was asking the Lord to make a way where she could earn extra money without sacrificing the children's security, and having the benefit of remaining home to raise our children. The Lord created a job for my wife in a position that never existed. The manager of a bus company whose office was on our campus one day called my wife to offer her a salary position equal to a bus driver. He asked if she would consider working as a baby sitter for one of the driver's children, and in doing this she could remain at home. She gladly accepted the offer and for the remaining time we spent at Bible College she was able to earn extra money, and still remain at home with our Children. He truly is our Provider!"

"And my God shall supply all your need according to His riches in glory by Christ Jesus." (Phil.4:19).

17

His Provisions Are
New Every Morning

As summer recess was fast approaching, we were well aware of our need to secure summer work to provide the necessary income. We brought this need to the Lord, and once again, He had gone before us to prepare the way. Our friends Jim and Irene had heard that we were in need of employment, so they invited us to spend the summer with them at their beautiful home in Long Island, while I worked with my friend Jim. It worked out perfectly; our families were very close, and we enjoyed a wonderful summer of fellowship! Jim and Irene also had a built in pool, so this occupied most of our children's time each day. It turned out to be one of our families most memorable summers!

The following year during summer break the Lord

provided me with a great connection. A Pastor from Connecticut offered me a position to be his assistant Pastor, and serve in ministry with him. This not only provided us with income, but also needed experience. Once again, He is FAITHFUL!

Our last year upon graduation, we found ourselves in need of a position, in the ministry. And also, we were required to leave the apartment upon graduation. We had not received any ministry offers, and we were beginning to get concerned. Having learned from passed experiences, we went to the Lord for help. And of course, He made a way where there was no way. How? One day, I received a call from the college President, who invited me to his office. I shared our dilemma and my concerns with him, and God gave us favor with this man. He simply made a call to a friend while I was present, and this provided me the opportunity to candidate (try out for the position) for the Church in New Jersey. Now again, we see the hand of the Lord. And we shall see His hand on countless occasions as He provided and made a way for us. "Declaring the end from the beginning..." (Is. 46:10).

18

OUR FIRST CHURCH

W e made our way to this church in New Jersey since the opportunity was made available to us to candidate (try out for the position). After conducting the church service that Sunday, we found out that the congregation and church board members loved us, it was unanimous, they elected me to serve as their Pastor.

Our new challenge was now to find a parsonage (home in which the church provides for their Pastor and family). The church had a small congregation with little or no resources. Therefore, they were in no position to help us. And we were in no position to rent or purchase a house. Besides, rental for a family of six was not available. While we faced this dilemma, we were still in transition from our apartment at the campus to the Church each Sunday, which was a several hour drive. But the Lord, once again, had gone before us.

One Sunday during a service, we were sharing our need for a house. There happened to be a young woman who was visiting our service. She turned to her mother and said she wanted to donate toward the purchase of our house. Suddenly, the Holy Spirit began to inspire all of the people there to give generously. Let me mention that this was a small congregation of people yet they continued to give even after we had returned to our apartment at the college campus. "This was the Lord's doing, and it is marvelous in our eyes."

Shortly thereafter, we received a call to notify us of the good news. To our pleasant surprise, not only were the people inspired to give in this time of need, but amazingly the amount was sufficient for a down payment on a house at that time. Truly, He goes before us to make a way where there is no way. He said: "I will never leave you nor forsake you." (Heb.13:5). This is something we certainly discovered from our past experiences, His Word is true.

19

MOVING FORWARD

As time went on, the Lord began to prepare us for our next step in ministry. One day, I received a call from our District Superintendent of our denomination who offered me an opportunity to candidate at one of their other churches in New Jersey. After seeking the Lord for direction, my wife and I both felt good in our hearts about this and we accepted the invitation to candidate (try out for) the new position as Senior Pastor. We were invited to the church to preach, and become acquainted with the Board members, as well as the congregation. Shortly after, to our delight, I was offered the position as Senior Pastor. Enthusiastically, we put our house up for sale and relocated from North Jersey to South Jersey.

Everything fell nicely into place. Fortunately, this time, the Church provided a nice Parsonage for our family to live in which was conveniently situated next to the Church building. This began a whole new adventure which lasted more than 21 years serving as Senior Pastor, and another door opened as well to serve as the Gloucester County Police Chaplain which was a great avenue to reach, serve, and minister to many people outside of our church!!

20

A VISION COMING TO PASS

Having now settled in and serving as Senior Pastor and enjoying the responsibilities, we began to see the need for an educational building including a Day Care-Nursery and eventually including K–5th grade.

Now this plan was revealed to my wife while we were resident at the Bible College campus seven years prior. And it was revealed to her in the following way: In an open vision, she saw herself in our home sitting at the table with Jesus. He said to her, "Bake me some bread." She said, "I don't know how Lord, but I'll find someone who can." Suddenly, a blue print was revealed to her and a floor plan that had many rooms in a school building.

Fast forward seven years, and we were now situated in a church where I was Senior Pastor, and we found ourselves planning to build an educational building attached to the church. Moreover, after we had the plans designed and drawn up by an Architect, we discovered that it was the same layout which my wife received in a vision from the Lord! "For the vision is yet for an appointed time, but in the end it will speak, and it will not lie. Though it tarries, wait for it; because it will surely come, it will not tarry." (Habakkuk 2:3).

21

BUILDING PROGRAM

Now that we had the plans completed and the Church Board approval, we had to raise the money for construction. "Unless the LORD builds the house, they labor in vain who build it..." (Psm.127:1).

Consequently, I presented the building plan to our congregation. Unfortunately, some were opposed while others were very supportive. Some had the vision to build an educational facility that would introduce many children to our Lord as well as receiving a Christian Education. The opposition would argue that it was not affordable. However, in the natural this might be true. But, in the spiritual, we were reminded of my wife's vision which encouraged us to "be steadfast, immovable, always abounding in the work of the Lord, knowing that your labor is not in vain in the Lord" (1 Cor.15:58).

Thereafter, we promoted our Building Fund each

Sunday; our people began to give. It became very apparent that the Lord was in this project as His people gave generously, and from their hearts. "So let each one give as he purposes in his heart, not grudgingly or of necessity; for God loves a cheerful giver" (2 Corinthians 9:7).

It wasn't long before we had raised a substantial amount for a deposit on a loan that would make it possible to begin construction and to complete it. And though I wasn't in favor of a loan, we agreed to it.

With great anticipation construction had begun and surprisingly, it was completed within a year. There was great rejoicing and celebration on the day we dedicated our building to the Lord!

Now in the midst of construction and other responsibilities within the church, we discovered that we were growing not only as a congregation, but more than that as a family, and a fellowship.

And yes, like many churches, we had our trials and disappointments over the course of 21 plus years. However, reflecting on our time as Senior Pastor, and Herborg, Director of our Christian School. It was truly a wonderful adventure of faith; a foundation upon which my Wife and I, along with our four children had hands-on experience. Yes, we were in the "School of Christ" and the Teacher was none other than the Holy Spirit. Also, it was a season for us to develop our spiritual gifts and prepare us for our next assignment from the Lord. "Who has believed our report? And to whom has the arm of the Lord been revealed?" (Is.53:1). All Glory to His Wonderful Name!!!

22

TO THE NATIONS

Having served for more than 21 years as Senior Pastor, the Lord was now calling us into our next chapter in ministry...to the Nations. "Go into all the world and preach the Gospel to every creature..." (Mark.16:15).

Since that time, we have ministered in Countries such as Africa, Canada, Greenland, Ireland, Macedonia, Mexico, Norway and across the USA. We have shared the Good News to the multitudes in churches, crusades, conferences, tent meetings, and street corners. We have seen the sick healed, blind see, the lame walk, deaf hear, and mute speak, as the gospel was faithfully preached to many from all different walks of life.

God's plan for salvation also includes physical healing! Yes, the major emphasis is winning the lost. But, He died for our sins and sicknesses!!! Healing originated with

God—it wasn't man's idea. It's in the plan of redemption. The scriptures bear this truth. Jesus never denied anyone from receiving healing. "He healed all who came to HIM! Jesus Christ is the same, yesterday, today, and forever." (Hebrews 13:8).

Some testimonies of God's healing power, and miraculous work among the people:

1. A deaf and mute senior woman healed and delivered. She can now hear and speak!

2. A child from a family of nine received her sight. Her mother testifies.

3. A senior man received his sight.

4. A deaf and mute woman, 26 yrs. of age, received her hearing and began to shout "Jesus healed me, Jesus healed me!"

5. A young woman was healed from a withered hand.

6. A man was bitten by a poisonous snake, his doctor warned him that if he didn't come in, and if he was not treated, he would die. He came to our meeting to receive healing and was instantly healed!

7. A woman was unable to have children. She came up and asked us to pray and believe God with her that she would be able to have children. A year later when we returned to minister there, she attended the meeting with her husband and baby. All Glory to God!!!

These are just some of the miraculous healings which I have witnessed as God powerfully demonstrated His love to all those we reached out to. We continue to work with the local Pastors here in the States, churches in Macedonia, as well as southern Mexico. This includes both Evangelism and Missions, reaching people from all walks of life both in the city and outskirts. To this day as I continue on this glorious journey and adventure of Faith, I can still emphatically say, "Where He leads I will follow!" All glory to our God and Savior Jesus Christ who has done great things in the midst of us!!!

The following pages are pictures of just a few of my many adventures of faith that I have experienced from following the Lord.

Blind girl comes up with her Mother to testify she can now SEE!!

*Preparing the Celebration Feast with some
of the local church members*

Preaching, Teaching, & Healing

An eager crowd listening to God's word preached

*Praying over the people who are desperate
for an encounter with God's power*

Blind man comes up to testify "I was once blind, but now can SEE!!"

Woman who was barren (she would never have children) had come up for prayer a year previously. The following year she returned with her husband, and "Miracle Baby"!!

Man was told he would die from a poisonous snake
bite. He came up for prayer, and in the picture
he is standing next to me alive and well!

CONCLUSION

It has been a joy following the Lord. Through it all, we have learned to trust HIM in spite of our feelings and sometimes doubts, and uncertainties. Truly, God has demonstrated that He will never leave us nor forsake us. His loving hand has kept us from falling. God has proven time and again to be our Provider, Healer, and Sustainer. He is a friend who sticks closer than a brother.

We desire for the church and the skeptic to know that our God is faithful, and when He calls you He doesn't abandon you. Yes, God will at times test your faith but if you persevere you will be victorious. He knows "the end from the beginning", and every step that you take with the Lord will lead you one step closer to your final destination. AMEN!

You might ask: "How do I begin this relationship with God?" It begins by confessing Jesus Christ as your personal Lord and Savior. Invite Jesus into your heart. He will forgive your sins, and you will then become "born again," a child of God, with a new start in life. (John 3:16, 2 Cor. 5:17)

Congratulations, your new life has just begun. Now go, and begin your new journey...Where He leads, <u>you</u> will follow!!!

FOUNDATIONAL PRINCIPLES FROM GOD'S WORD (NUGGETS OF TRUTH)

The next few pages are nuggets that will help to build and encourage your Faith for your everyday walk with the Lord. These nuggets will include: **Faith, God's Unconditional Love, Christ in Me, Basic Truths that Apply to Prayer, You Have Not Because You Ask Not, & The Resurrection.**

1. Faith: What kind of Faith do you have?

For the benefit of many who desire to follow the Lord, I will include the principles of faith which I have gleaned throughout my ministry. The faith walk isn't always easy, but always challenging! It will lead you down a path which you have not gone before. Faith without corresponding actions is dead but you will always come out on top! "Faith is the victory that overcomes the world." (1Jn.5:4).

There are two kinds of faith. Thomas faith, and Abraham faith. What's the difference between Thomas's faith and Abraham's? Thomas's faith does not measure up. He is called "doubting Thomas" in John 20:27 NIV. Notice, Jesus does not commend Thomas's faith (Jn. 20: 24-29). Thomas believed circumstances instead of the Word of God. Doubt and unbelief instinctively base everything on what it sees or what it feels. Jesus said you are blessed when you believe and have not seen.

Abraham's faith was based on the promise. (Rom.4:17- 21). Abraham believed what God spoke to him about something he could not see. The natural mind or circumstances said to Abraham you will never receive God's promise. You could not have children when you were young, so what makes you think you can have a child now that you are over 100 years old? Abraham chose to believe, to have faith in that which was spoken to him, instead of what the circumstances told him. Abraham was called the friend of God.

Notice: Faith begins where the will of God is known…

Let this fact settle deep down in your heart!!!

Please note: We have the same kind of faith as Abraham.

(Gal.3:7-9). Someone once said, "You can't have Abraham's blessing with the Thomas kind of faith."

Do you know that faith will not keep trouble away from you? But it will cause you to triumph over it.

It has been said "Great faith comes out of great tests."

And, "Great victories come out of great battles."

2. God's Unconditional Love

We find God's great unconditional love displayed in the story of the Parable of the Prodigal Son. Luke 15:11-32 (NIV) says: [11] "There was a man who had two sons. [12] The younger one said to his father, 'Father, give me my share of the estate.' So he divided his property between them. [13] "Not long after that, the younger son got together all he had, set off for a distant country and there squandered his wealth in wild living. [14] After he had spent everything, there was a severe famine in that whole country, and he began to be in need. [15] So he went and hired himself out to a citizen of that country, who sent him to his fields to feed pigs. [16] He longed to fill his stomach with the pods that the pigs were eating, but no one gave him anything. [17] "When he came to his senses, he said, 'How many of my father's hired servants have food to spare, and here I am starving to death! [18] I will set out and go back to my father and say to him: Father, I have sinned against heaven and against you. [19] I am no longer worthy to be called your son; make me like one of your hired servants.' ²⁰ So he got up and went to his father.

"But while he was still a long way off, his father saw him and was filled with compassion for him; he ran to his son, threw his arms around him and kissed him. ²¹ "The son said to him, 'Father, I have sinned against heaven and against you. I am no longer worthy to be called your son.' ²² "But the father said to his servants, 'Quick! Bring the best robe and put it on him. Put a ring on his finger and sandals on his feet. ²³ Bring the fattened calf and kill it. Let's have a feast and celebrate. ²⁴ For this son of mine was dead and is alive again; he was lost and is found.' So they began to celebrate. ²⁵ "Meanwhile, the older son was in the field. When he came near the house, he heard music and dancing. ²⁶ So he called one of the servants and asked him what was going on. ²⁷ 'Your brother has come,' he replied, 'and your father has killed the fattened calf because he has him back safe and sound.' ²⁸ "The older brother became angry and refused to go in. So his father went out and pleaded with him. ²⁹ But he answered his father, 'Look! All these years I've been slaving for you and never disobeyed your orders. Yet you never gave me even a young goat so I could celebrate with my friends. ³⁰ But when this son of yours who has squandered your property with prostitutes comes home, you kill the fattened calf for him!' ³¹ "My son," the father said, 'you are always with me, and everything I have is yours. ³² But we had to celebrate and be glad, because this brother of yours was dead and is alive again; he was lost and is found.'

The son heard His Father whisper to him "All I have is yours." This demonstrates how the love of God is unconditional, without strings attached. Our love for the Lord is often shown by our obedience to HIM. But, His love is evident by His giving. You cannot divorce God's love from His provision. Do you know He has given to us all things freely to enjoy? You cannot know Him as a loving God until you see Him as a giving God! The problem is, very few Christians take what belongs to them. Very few Christians appropriate what God has freely offered.

Please note: God's love did not depend on our loving Him!!! God loved us even while we were far from Him in every way. The scripture reminds us of His love: "But God demonstrates His own *love* toward us in that while we were still sinners, Christ died for us." (Rom.5:8) (1Jn.4:10). "He brought me to His banqueting table and His banner over me is *love*." This truth is revealed in the story of The Prodigal Son. It clearly reveals God's Love for us, His unconditional Love!!! It unlocks the mystery of His abundant grace which He has freely poured out upon the human race through His Son the Lord Jesus Christ.

3. Christ in Me

1Cor.3:16-17; 6:19-20

There are several subjects which every believer should major in. We need to major in the New Birth, and learn what IN CHRIST MEANS.

Stop dwelling on who you *were*, rather, dwell on who you *are*. You may be living in the same body, you may have some scars from the past. But, your Spirit is brand new on the inside (2Cor.5:17).

As a Christian, your sins are forgiven (1Jn. 1:9). You don't have to make a deal with God. It's a gift! If you had to pay for it, then it ceases to be a gift. It's not based on what we did, but on what Christ did.

It's not a matter of what church you belong to. It's a matter of which family you belong to. There are two families on earth. (natural and spiritual).

When you're in the family of God, you are an heir of God, and Joint heirs with Jesus Christ. We share equally with Christ in His inheritance. Therefore, you have all the rights and privileges as a son (Rom.8:16-17). Your redemptive rights have not been put on hold for heaven. What does God's word say? "Now we are the sons of God..."(1Jn.3:2). Everything you need belongs to you.

Another subject that correlates with *Christ in Me* that we need to learn what the Bible says about is: The Indwelling of the Holy Spirit (1Cor.3:16). In the New Covenant, we find three relations that God sustains with men: "God for us, God with us, and God in us." In the Old Testament God was for Israel and with Israel. But under the New Testament, God is in us! Now, to have

God *for us*, guarantees success. (Rom.8:31). To have God *with us*, you become utterly fearless. (Heb.13:5). To have God in us makes us more than "conquerors." And, we can do all things through Christ who strengthens us!!! In other words: With the Greater One in us, there can be no lack, and no lack of Power, AMEN!!!

4. Basic Truths that Apply to Prayer

"Men should always pray and never give up." These are the words of Jesus. You will find many scriptures which support this truth, or its equivalent. Eph.6:18, Jn.15:7, 1Jn. 5:14-15, Lk.18:1.

We are exhorted to "Pray without ceasing." Is it possible to pray without ceasing? Yes, it is an attitude of prayer carried throughout your walk with God. Decide what you want from God. Then find promises from God's Word to support your desire. Get these promises fixed in your heart, not just in your mind. Be ready to use them against the enemy.

"Whatever things you ask when you pray, believe that you receive them, and you will have them." (Mk11:24). Remember, the Bible is God's Word speaking to you. Let every thought and desire affirm that you have what you ask. Don't dwell on unbelief and doubt. Don't allow a mental picture of failure (Phil.4:8). If doubt persists, rebuke it, and resist it (1Pet.5:8-9).

Do not accept anything other than that for which you have asked. Be patient, God hears your prayer. "God may be late, but He is always on time!"

Avoid "friends" and yes, Churches who disagree with your walk of faith and who question the Word of God. Be sure to enjoy fellowship with those who contribute to your faith! Keep your mind occupied with God's Word. I remind you, doubt and unbelief is sin. It's called an evil report. (Num. 13:33). Meditate on the promises of God which support your request. (Prov.4:20-22). Make plans as though you see yourself as having the answer.

Note: To the natural mind, your request may seem impossible. However, the mind of faith says you have it! It belongs to you! Remain in an attitude of praise and thanksgiving for the answer is on the way! I remind you, faith without corresponding action is dead! (Jam.2:20).

"And whatever you do in word or deed, do all in the name of the Lord Jesus, giving thanks to God the Father through Him." (Colossians 3:17).

AMEN and AMEN!!!

5. You Have Not Because You Ask Not!

A miracle in the making describes this wonderful experience:

We were holding meetings in Macedonia. And, one night after the meeting, we took a taxi back to our room. As we arrived, I reached into my pocket for some money to pay the driver. In doing so, I placed my Bible and notes on the back seat.

When the taxi driver left us I realized at that moment that I forgot my Bible and notes in the taxi. I franticly cried out to my partner, "Oh no Dave, I left my Bible and notes in the taxi!" It seemed very definite that I had lost my Bible and notes for good. My heart cried out in despair, "Oh God!!"

Suddenly, the Lord said "pray." It appeared to be impossible at that moment to even consider praying and David expressed the same doubt on his facial expression. Nevertheless, we prayed a quick prayer as doubt raced across my mind: "Lord, have him return my Bible, Amen."

To my surprise, the taxi driver made a u-turn, pulled up in front of us, got out of the taxi, with a big smile he handed me my Bible, and left. He spoke no English.

This had taken place at night, and it was dark. The driver would not have noticed so quickly that the Bible was in the back seat. He could not have known whether we were still waiting at that street corner he dropped us off at. And yet, within five minutes after we had prayed the driver returned with my Bible and preaching notes!

Note: "God commands the impossible, and then makes it possible!" "All glory to God. He does all things well!!!"

6. Why the Resurrection?

1. As Christians, we know that God's plan of redemption was not fulfilled until Jesus was raised from the dead.

2. The reality of the resurrection is the central theme of the message of salvation. It is the foundation!

3. Virtually, every message preached by the disciples mention His resurrection. "He arose! He lives! But now Christ has been raised from the dead and declared the Son of God with Power." (1Cor. 15:20, Rom.1:4).

4. As a man Jesus completely stripped the devil of his power. "And Christ made a public display of demonic rulers and authorities having triumphed over them through Him." (Col.2:15). Satan was not only stripped of his legal authority but also of his weapons-- death, sickness, and poverty.

5. When Christ took his seat at the right hand of His Majesty, He proved once and for all that Satan's defeat was complete.

6. **Why the resurrection**? When Jesus burst forth from the prison of hell He ascended on high and led a host of prisoners (Eph. 4:8).

7. **Why the resurrection**? In the mind of God, every believer shares complete identity with Christ from the cross to the grave.

8. **Why the resurrection?** Jesus displayed the power of forgiveness. Jesus chose to die for every sinner so that we could be forgiven, and to assure eternal life to all who accept the gift of Salvation.

9. **Why the resurrection**? So Christ can declare to all that he is the RESURRECTION and the LIFE!!! And whoever believes in HIM should not perish but have eternal LIFE! (Jo. 11:25-26).

10. Lastly, **because of the resurrection** millions of lives have been transformed and changed from that glorious day, until now! The resurrection power of Jesus Christ is in every believer. Because Jesus lives in us, we are able to minister to others resulting in giving hope to the hopeless, deliverance to the addict, healing to the sick, and restoring the lives of those who are lost.

Further Reading

How You Can be Led by the Spirit of God
Kenneth E. Hagin

Plans, Purposes, and Pursuits
Kenneth E. Hagin

**What to do When Faith seems
Weak and Victory Lost**
Kenneth E. Hagin

The Touch of God
Rodney M. Howard-Browne

Living a Life of Fire
Reinhard Bonnke

Healing the Sick
T.L. Osborn

Christ the Healer
F.F. Bosworth

The Blood and the Glory
Billye Brim